10/03

20.95

THE FOUNDERS
OF FAMOUS
FOOD COMPANIES

The *Collective Biographies* Series

—Collective Biographies—

THE FOUNDERS OF FAMOUS FOOD COMPANIES

Barbara Kramer

Enslow Publishers, Inc.

40 Industrial Road	PO Box 38
Box 398	Aldershot
Berkeley Heights, NJ 07922	Hants GU12 6BP
USA	UK

http://www.enslow.com

Library of Congress Cataloging-in-Publication Data

Kramer, Barbara.
    The founders of famous food companies / Barbara Kramer.
        p. cm. — (Collective biographies)
    Includes bibliographical references and index.
    ISBN 0-7660-1537-8 (hardcover)
    1. Food industry and trade—United States—Biography—Juvenile literature.
    2. Philanthropists—United States—Biography—Juvenile literature. 3. Brand
name products—United States—Juvenile literature. I. Title. II. Series.
HD9009.8 .K73 2001
338.7'664'0092273—dc21

                                 2001000222

[B]

Printed in the United States of America

10 9 8 7 6 5 4 3 2 1

To Our Readers:
We have done our best to make sure all Internet addresses in this book were active and
appropriate when we went to press. However, the author and the publisher have no
control over and assume no liability for the material available on those Internet sites
or on other Web sites they may link to. Any comments or suggestions can be sent by
e-mail to comments@enslow.com or to the address on the back cover.

Every effort has been made to locate all copyright holders of material used in this
book. If any errors or omissions have occurred, corrections will be made in future
editions of this book.

Illustration Credits: Associated Press AP, p. 90; Ben & Jerry's Homemade, p. 82; Fotos
Inter./Munawar Hosain/Archive Photos, p. 92; Hershey Community Archives, pp. 10,
16; Kellogg Co. Inc., p. 20; KFC Enterprises Inc., pp. 46, 50; Library of Congress,
pp.24, 98; McDonalds Corporation, pp. 38, 41; Mrs. Fields Inc., pp. 74, 80;
Pepperidge Farm Inc., pp. 28, 33; SAGA/Frank Capri/Archive Photos, p. 71; Uncle
Wally's, p.64; Wendy's International, Inc., pp. 56, 60.

Cover Illustrations: Mrs. Fields Inc.; Pepperidge Farm Inc.; SAGA/Frank
Capri/Archive Photos; Wendy's International, Inc.

Contents

Preface

At one time chocolate was a luxury in the United States, affordable only for the rich. There was no such thing as cereal flakes or fast-food restaurants. Our eating habits have changed, however, and the people profiled here were part of those changes. These are the stories of the men and women behind some of the country's most famous food names.

It was Milton S. Hershey who made chocolate available to everyone when he began mass-producing his milk-chocolate bar. W. K. Kellogg discovered cereal flakes by accident when he was experimenting to find a bread substitute. From that discovery he built the cereal empire that still bears his name.

In 1929, the stock market crashed, marking the beginning of the Great Depression—the most serious economic crisis in United States history. Banks closed and people lost their money. One out of every four people were unemployed, but Hershey and Kellogg each found ways to keep their employees working. During the Depression, Margaret Rudkin began manufacturing her homemade whole wheat bread, bringing much needed jobs to her community.

Fast food is now a regular part of our diets, but that was not the case in 1955 when Ray Kroc began franchising the McDonald's Restaurants. Under that arrangement, other people paid for the right to operate their own McDonald's Restaurants the

McDonald's way. Colonel Harland Sanders, founder of Kentucky Fried Chicken, and Dave Thomas, founder of Wendy's Restaurants, have added their own special touches to the fast-food franchise industry.

Wally Amos has been called "the father of the gourmet chocolate chip cookie."[1] He founded his Famous Amos Chocolate Chip Cookie Company in 1975. Two years later, Debbi Fields, a twenty-year-old housewife with no business experience, made her own mark on the gourmet cookie business.

Ben Cohen and Jerry Greenfield introduced a new business style when they began manufacturing their Ben & Jerry's ice cream in 1978. They believed that work should be fun. They also believed in sharing their prosperity. They made it a company policy stating that 7.5 percent of their before-tax profits would go to charity. Paul Newman took that idea one step further when he founded Newman's Own food company in 1982. One hundred percent of the company's after-tax profits go to charity.

The people profiled here come from a variety of backgrounds. Some of them had only an elementary school education. Some started their companies with little knowledge about how to run a business.

A number of them were told that their ideas would never work, but that did not keep them from trying. In fact, some experienced more than one business failure. "I learn more from my mistakes," Debbi Fields has said. "That's one secret of my success."[2]

For some of these men and women, opportunities were a long time coming. W. K. Kellogg and Margaret Rudkin were in their forties when they first enjoyed their manufacturing success. Ray Kroc was fifty-two when he opened his first McDonald's Restaurant. Colonel Harland Sanders was sixty-six when he began selling his Kentucky Fried Chicken franchises.

There is no one way to start a business as these people demonstrate. Their stories are as unique as the individuals themselves. But they have each made their mark on our culture and the way we eat.

Milton S. Hershey

Milton S. Hershey
Pioneer of the Chocolate Bar

Milton S. Hershey's early attempts to start a candy-making business were not successful, but he learned from his mistakes. In 1900, he became a millionaire as a manufacturer of caramel candy. But it was chocolate that later brought him fame and even greater fortune.

Milton was born on September 13, 1857, on a farm near Derry Church, Pennsylvania. His father, Henry Hershey, was a dreamer who tried a variety of jobs hoping to make his fortune. None of them ever quite worked out. But it was Henry Hershey who gave his son his first business advice. "If you want to make money, you must do things in a very big way," he said.[1] Milton's mother, Fannie Hershey, the daughter of a Mennonite minister, taught Milton the value of hard work.

The family moved often as Henry Hershey went from job to job. Each time, Milton had to change schools. He quit school at thirteen and began an apprenticeship with Sam Ernst, the editor of a small weekly newspaper in Gap, Pennsylvania. Milton did not like the work, nor the fact that Ernst had a bad temper. Ernst called Milton clumsy and yelled at him often. One day Milton's hat fell on the press while the paper was being printed and Ernst fired him on the spot. "I lost my job when I let my old straw hat fall on the form rollers—which I may have done on purpose," Hershey recalled.[2]

He soon began another apprenticeship working as a candymaker for Joseph H. Royer in Lancaster, Pennsylvania. Hershey spent four years as an apprentice for Royer. Then in 1876, when he was eighteen years old, he decided that it was time to go into business for himself. The United States was celebrating one hundred years of independence that year. As part of the celebration, the city of Philadelphia was hosting a world's fair. Hershey set up shop in Philadelphia hoping to benefit from the large amount of tourists attending the fair.

From the beginning, Hershey struggled to make ends meet. Stores bought his candy on credit, meaning they paid for the candy at a later time. But Hershey had to pay cash when he bought the sugar to make his candy. Hershey had to borrow money from relatives to keep the business going. Finally, in 1882, faced with too many bills, Hershey closed the candy business.

He then joined his father in Colorado where Henry Hershey was working in the silver mines. Milton Hershey got a job as an assistant to a candy-maker in Denver. After little success in Colorado, Henry Hershey went to Chicago. Milton Hershey went with his father and set up a candy-making business there. It lasted only a short time.

Milton Hershey made another attempt at a candy-making business in New York City. When that one also failed, he returned to Lancaster and tried again. This time he specialized in making caramels. He used fresh milk for his caramels, a secret he had learned from the candymaker in Denver. His big break came when a candy importer from England visited the factory and placed a large order. After that, the business grew rapidly. The Lancaster Caramel Company became one of the largest businesses in the community.

In 1893, Hershey visited the World's Columbian Exposition, a world's fair in Chicago. He was fascinated with one of the exhibits—chocolate-making machinery from Germany. Hershey returned to that exhibit each day of the fair to learn more about the difficult job of making chocolate. When the fair closed, Hershey bought the equipment and moved it to Lancaster. He began manufacturing chocolate in a corner of the caramel factory.

On a sales trip to a candy store in Jamestown, New York, Hershey met Catherine "Kitty" Sweeney, a salesclerk at the store. They were married in New York City in May 1898. Hershey was forty years old and Sweeney was twenty-five.

In 1900, Hershey sold his caramel business to the American Caramel Company of Philadelphia for $1 million. He and his wife and mother then left for a tour around the world. They got as far as Mexico City when they decided that they were tired of traveling. They returned home and Hershey went back to making chocolate.

One of his projects was to develop his own formula for milk chocolate. Milk chocolate had been discovered in Switzerland and was popular in Europe. In the United States milk chocolate was hand-made and only the rich could afford it. Hershey wanted to make it available to everyone through mass production—using machinery to manufacture large quantities, which brought the cost of the product down. Hershey experimented until he found just the right ingredients for his milk chocolate. In 1903, he began selling a five-cent milk chocolate bar with the name Hershey imprinted on it.

That same year Hershey broke ground for a new factory to manufacture his chocolate. He wanted to build the factory in the country where he would have access to the fresh milk used in his chocolates. Earlier, Hershey had repurchased the family homestead in Derry Church where he was born, and he decided to build there.

Hershey's financial advisers told him that his plan would not work. Where would he get employees? There was nowhere for them to live in Derry Church. But Hershey had a much larger plan—he would build a town.

He began by building houses where employees could live and stores where they could shop. He built a trolley system so that people who did not want to live in the town could commute from cities in the area. He added parks, a bank, and set aside land for churches.

In 1906, a contest was held to decide on a name for the town. The winner was "Hersheykoko." However, at the request of the U.S. Post Office, the name was shortened to Hershey.

Hershey was not involved with the day-to-day operations of the factory. He spent much of his time experimenting with new products and expanding the town. He also opened a school for orphan boys. He later explained why the school was for boys only. "The orphan boy has a harder time than anybody else, you know. There are always relatives or outsiders to take an orphan girl," he said.[3]

The Hershey Industrial School had been Kitty Hershey's idea. Both of the Hersheys loved children, but had never had any of their own. The school was built on a farm because Hershey wanted the boys to learn about hard work the way he had working on

Hershey poses with students from the school for orphan boys that he founded. The school was built on a farm because Hershey wanted the boys to learn about hard work the same way he did.

the farm. They received their schooling there and also learned a trade.

Kitty Hershey died in 1915 after a long illness. Three years later Hershey donated his shares of Hershey stock to the school. Hershey was a private man and the donation was made quietly. It was five years before even the people of Hershey found out about his generosity. On November 9, 1923, *The New York Times* ran an article about the transfer of the stock that was valued at $60 million.

Surprisingly, Hershey never advertised his chocolate products. The business grew by word of mouth. "We turned out the best chocolate we could make," he explained, "and the business just grew by itself."[4]

As times changed, Hershey made business adjustments. During World War I, it was difficult for him to find the sugar he needed for his chocolate. In 1916, he bought sugarcane fields in Cuba and began refining sugar. Much as he had done in Pennsylvania, he built a whole town in Cuba and named it Central Hershey.

In 1929, the stock market crashed bringing the start of the Great Depression. To keep his employees working, Hershey began another large building program in Hershey. Men, who had worked in the factory, now worked on construction. During that time Hershey built a community building that had a theater, a gymnasium, a swimming pool, and a library. He built a resort hotel, a sports arena for ice hockey, and a football stadium. He also built a windowless, air-conditioned office. The climate-controlled building was one of the first of its kind. Hershey looked back on that time with pride. "No man in Hershey was dropped by reason of the Depression," he noted.[5]

During World War II, the U.S. government asked Hershey to develop a high-energy chocolate bar that soldiers could carry in their pockets for emergencies. It needed to be a type of chocolate that would not melt. Hershey, who was then eighty-four years old, put his chemists to work creating a bar called "Field Ration D." The factory produced 500,000 bars a day, and the company received a special award from the government for that effort.

Hershey lived to see the end of the war, but died a couple of months later on October 13, 1945. Today, the Hershey Industrial School, now called the Milton S. Hershey School, serves about one thousand boys and girls from kindergarten through twelfth grade. Most of the students come from needy families primarily in inner-city areas. They live on the school grounds and receive a free education. The Hershey Foods Corporation is still a thriving industry and Hershey, Pennsylvania, is a popular tourist area. It's a lasting tribute to the man who built the town with chocolate.

2

W. K. Kellogg
The Discovery of Flaked Cereal

For much of his life, Will Keith (W. K.) Kellogg lived in the shadow of his older, more successful brother, Dr. John Harvey (J. H.) Kellogg. Dr. Kellogg was a gifted surgeon and the superintendent of the famous Battle Creek Sanitarium in Battle Creek, Michigan. The San, as it was called, was similar to today's health resorts. People went there to receive natural treatments for their illnesses. Therapies included mineral baths, rest, fresh air, exercise, and a strict vegetarian diet.

Dr. Kellogg ran the medical end of the business. W. K. Kellogg did almost everything else. He was the bookkeeper, clerk, errand boy, and custodian. But for all his work, his brother paid him very little. "I feel kind of blue," Kellogg once wrote in his journal. "Am

W. K. Kellogg

afraid that I will always be a poor man the way things look now."[1] Then in 1894, Kellogg made the discovery that would change his life.

W. K. Kellogg was born on April 7, 1860. He was a shy, serious-minded child, raised according to the strict religious beliefs of his parents. They were members of the Seventh-Day Adventists Church. Will was only seven years old when he went to work part-time at his father's broom factory. "I never learned to play," he recalled.[2]

In school he was labeled a slow learner. "The teacher thought I was dim-witted because I had difficulty reading what was on the blackboard," he explained.[3] At thirteen he dropped out of school and went to work full-time in his father's broom factory. By the time he was fourteen, he was a traveling broom salesman with his own sales territory.

It was not until Kellogg was an adult that he learned the real reason for his problems in school. He was nearsighted. He could not read what was on the blackboard because he could not see the words. He later enjoyed reading, and he was an eager learner. In 1880, he took a business course, completing the one-year course in only four months. That same year Kellogg married Ella Osborn Davis and began working for his brother at the sanitarium.

Dr. John Kellogg had taken over as superintendent of the Battle Creek Sanitarium in 1876. Until then, the Seventh-Day Adventists Church had managed the sanitarium. W. K. Kellogg worked long hours. "One year I kept a record of the number of hours I was on duty for the sanitarium. This record shows that one week I was on duty 120 hours," Kellogg noted.[4] Dr. Kellogg often rode his bicycle to work, while W. K. Kellogg ran alongside him getting his orders for the day. While the sanitarium grew, W. K. Kellogg's earnings did not. He worked at the sanitarium more than three years before receiving his first raise.

W. K. Kellogg did not like the way his brother treated him. He sometimes referred to himself as "J. H.'s flunky."[5] But he continued to work at the sanitarium to provide for his growing family. He and his wife had five children. One son died in infancy and another one when he was four years old. Two sons and a daughter survived.

Sometimes the brothers worked well together. An example was the research they did to improve the diets of the sanitarium's patients. One of the projects they worked on was a bread substitute. They made it by boiling wheat, grinding it, and serving it as granola. One day they were interrupted while they were working. Later, when they went back to the pot of boiled wheat, they discovered that something had happened to it. Moisture had collected in each of the wheat berries. When they rolled the dough, it crumbled into flakes, instead of coming out in a large sheet.

Dr. Kellogg wanted to grind the flakes for granola, but W. K. Kellogg convinced his brother to toast the flakes and serve them to the patients. The new flaked breakfast food was a hit. Patients wanted to continue eating it after they left the sanitarium. That led to mail-order requests. Dr. Kellogg founded the Sanitas Nut Food Company to handle the mail-order business and put his brother in charge.

The brothers could not agree on how to market the cereal. Dr. Kellogg wanted to sell it as a health food. W. K. Kellogg saw the huge possibilities in marketing it as a breakfast food for everyone. In the meantime, word about the new product spread and other companies were starting to manufacture cereal. Between 1902 and 1906, more than forty breakfast food companies were established in Battle Creek.

Convinced that his brother would never realize the marketing potential of the cereal, W. K. Kellogg struck out on his own. Other companies were man-ufacturing wheat-based cereals, but Kellogg had experimented with a corn-based product. In 1906, he founded the Battle Creek Toasted Corn Flake Company. The name was later changed to the Kellogg Company. The first product was Kellogg's Corn Flakes.

Kellogg's split from the sanitarium caused hard feelings between the brothers. They did not have anything to do with each other again after that.

A key to Kellogg's early success was a large news-paper and magazine advertising campaign. One ad declared that "Wednesday Is Wink Day in New York."[6] The ad promised a free box of cornflakes for every woman who winked at her grocer that day. The

These women are inspecting boxes of Kellogg's Corn Flakes. W. K. Kellogg founded the Battle Creek Toasted Corn Flake Company in 1906. It was later called the Kellogg Company.

ad was a bit scandalous for the time, but sales in the New York area took a jump. Shipments went from two railroad boxcars a month, to one railroad boxcar a day.

On July 4, 1907, fire destroyed the Kellogg factory. "The fire is of no consequence," Kellogg said. "You can't burn down what we have registered in the minds of the American woman."[7] Production continued in temporary quarters while Kellogg rebuilt.

Kellogg was so busy working that he did not spend much time with his family. It was something he regretted later, especially when his wife died in 1912. Six years later, on January 1, 1918, he married Carrie Staines, a physician at the sanitarium.

Kellogg was a pioneer in labor relations. Factory workers traditionally worked ten hours a day. However, soon after Kellogg founded his manufacturing plant, he reduced his worker's hours to eight a day. He also provided a nursery for the children of women employees and medical and dental care.

During the Depression in the 1930s, Kellogg's business flourished, while other cereal companies were not doing as well. Kellogg's strategy was to increase advertising. Other companies were cutting back on advertising in order to reduce their operating expenses.

Kellogg also set up a plan for employees to work six hours a day. The day was divided into four, six-hour shifts, which kept the company's 2,000 employees working throughout the Depression.

Although the employees worked six-hour days, they were paid for eight hours.

He was also one of the first to move into the international market. In 1914, he began selling his products in Canada and England. In 1924, he built a cereal plant in Sydney, Australia, and in 1938 he built a plant in Manchester, England. Kellogg served as president of the company until 1939 when he became chairman of the board.

In 1943, J. H. Kellogg wrote a letter to his brother apologizing for the way he had treated him as an employee at the sanitarium. Unfortunately, the delivery of the letter was delayed. By the time W. K. Kellogg received it, his brother had died.

Kellogg's second wife died in 1948. The following year Kellogg resigned as chairman of the board. At that time the company posted annual sales of $80 million.

Kellogg believed that it was wrong for some people to enjoy great wealth while others lived in poverty, so he found ways to help others. He invested in a building program in Battle Creek that included founding two schools. One was the Ann J. Kellogg School for handicapped children, named after his mother. He also built a civic auditorium, a youth recreation center, an airport, and two hotels.

His one hobby was raising Arabian horses. In 1925, he bought a ranch in Pomona, California, near Los Angeles. Seven years later, he donated the ranch and his herd of Arabian horses to the University of

California. The ranch was to be used for research and teaching animal husbandry. Kellogg donated $600,000 to get that program started.

The biggest share of his fortune went to the W. K. Kellogg Foundation, which he founded in 1930. The foundation funds health, education, leadership, and agricultural projects, and supports programs to benefit children.

In his later years, Kellogg suffered from an eye disease called glaucoma. A characteristic of the disease is increased pressure on the eyeball. The pressure gradually causes a loss of sight. Although Kellogg was almost totally blind, he continued to work for the foundation until shortly before his death on October 6, 1951. He was ninety-one years old.

Today, the Kellogg Company produces over fifty different cereals, with manufacturing plants in twenty different countries. Kellogg's charitable work continues through the W. K. Kellogg Foundation. It is one of the largest charitable organizations of its kind.

Margaret Rudkin

Margaret Rudkin
An Old-fashioned Idea

Margaret Rudkin said that she was probably an example of the way "a business should not be started."[1] When she began selling her homemade bread, she had no training in running a manufacturing company. She was a homemaker with little money to invest in a business. At a time when people wanted white bread, she began selling whole wheat bread. "If I had talked to experts in our line of business in 1937, I would never have begun," Rudkin noted.[2] But she did not talk to the experts and her business grew faster than anyone could have imagined.

Margaret, the daughter of Joseph J. and Margaret Fogarty, was born in New York City on September 14, 1897. When Margaret was twelve, the family, which included five children, moved to Flushing, New York.

Margaret was a bright, energetic redhead who graduated at the top of her high school class. She then went to work as a bookkeeper at a bank in Flushing. "The bank had only ten employees, and until I came along, it had never hired a woman," she recalled.[3] After two years she became a teller at the bank, a position she liked because it gave her a chance to talk to people.

In 1919, she got a job at an investment company in New York City. There, she met Henry Rudkin, a partner in the firm. They were married on April 8, 1923. For the first five years of their marriage, they lived in New York City. Then, in 1928, they bought land near Fairfield, Connecticut, where they built a home. Henry Rudkin was a polo player, and he also built stables for his ten ponies.

They called their new home Pepperidge Farm, named after the pepperidge trees that grew on their land. They moved into their home in 1929, shortly before the stock market crashed and the Great Depression began. Henry Rudkin continued to go to his office in New York City each day, but with the state of the economy, there was not much work for an investment broker.

Margaret Rudkin began baking whole wheat bread for her family after the youngest of their three sons was diagnosed with asthma. Asthma causes breathing problems and is often triggered by allergies. The doctor suggested that a move to Arizona might help. The climate was dry there and the pollution level was low. Unfortunately, money was tight because of the Depression, and the family could not consider such a move.

Rudkin thought that a different diet might help her son. She did some research, learning that whole wheat flour was rich in Vitamin B and calcium, both of which were important to a healthy diet. She decided she would make her own bread using stone-ground whole-wheat flour. She remembered eating her grandmother's homemade bread when she was young. However, she had never watched her grandmother bake bread and had not learned how it was done.

Rudkin's early baking attempts were not encouraging. "That first loaf should have been sent to the Smithsonian Institute as a sample of bread from the Stone Age for it was as hard as rock and about one inch high," she recalled.[4] She had to learn how to work with yeast, which is what makes the bread rise. She continued to experiment and finally came up with bread that her family liked. Her son's health improved.

Rudkin told her son's doctor that she was baking bread using stone-ground whole-wheat flour. He did not believe that her family would eat it. He said that surely she needed to add at least some white flour for taste. Rudkin said her whole wheat bread tasted just fine and she took the doctor a sample. He liked it so much that he ordered more bread for himself and recommended it to some of his other patients.

Rudkin asked her doctor to write a letter endorsing the bread. With a copy of the letter and a sample of her bread, Rudkin visited other doctors. They bought her bread for themselves and recommended it to their patients.

At that time commercially-baked white bread was ten cents a loaf. Manufacturers kept the price down by mass-producing the bread—making large amounts by machine. Rudkin's homemade bread was twenty-five cents a loaf, more than twice what other bakeries were charging. Other bakers told her that people would not pay that much. "They will, if the loaf is worth twenty-five cents," she said, and she soon proved she was right.[5]

Rudkin's best sales tool was the bread itself. In the fall of 1937, she took a basket with eight loaves of whole wheat bread into town and asked the local grocer if he would sell it in his store. The grocer did not think the bread would sell, but Rudkin convinced him to try when she gave him a sample. By the time Rudkin arrived home, the grocer had already called saying that the bread was sold and he placed an order for more. Soon, other grocers in the area called and said that they wanted to carry the bread too.

In the beginning Rudkin baked the bread in her kitchen. When the orders increased, she hired a neighbor woman to help her and moved her business into the family's garage. By October 1937, after

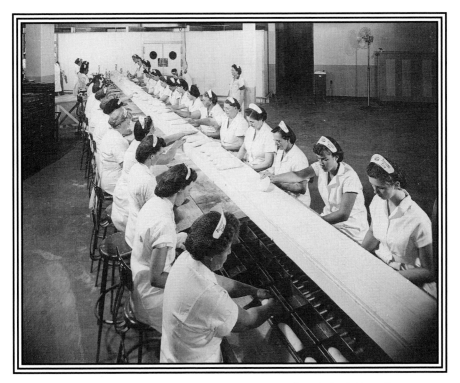

Employees at Pepperidge Farm, Inc. prepare bread for baking by kneading it to distribute the yeast evenly. Although other companies at the time kneaded their bread by running it through steel rollers, Rudkin employed women who kneaded the bread by hand.

being in business only two months, Rudkin had six employees and the company was producing one hundred loaves a day. In November she added a new product to her line—white bread for people who preferred it but still wanted the quality of homemade bread.

Rudkin's business soon outgrew her garage, but she had plenty of room to expand. Her husband had been badly injured in a fall from a horse in 1932. That brought an end to his riding and polo playing. Rudkin converted the empty stables for her business.

The United States was in the midst of the Great Depression at the time and unemployment was high. The city welcomed the new job opportunities her company provided and gave Rudkin special permission to run her business on private property. The company not only provided work for the employees of Pepperidge Farm, but it also created jobs at the mills that ground the whole wheat flour and the companies that provided the other ingredients. By 1939 Rudkin became the only customer of a local dairy, whose daily output went to providing fresh milk for her bread.

In 1940, Rudkin expanded again moving into rented space in Norwalk, Connecticut. It was meant to be a short-term arrangement. However, with the outbreak of World War II, she ended up staying in that location longer than planned. Some of the products that she needed to make her bread were hard to get during the war. Rudkin preferred to cut back on production rather than sacrifice quality.

The war ended in 1945, and two years later Rudkin moved into a new $625,000 factory. The factory was capable of producing four thousand loaves of bread an hour. By that time Rudkin was using some mass-producing methods, such as machines to package the bread. However, she still employed women who kneaded the bread by hand. The purpose of kneading is to distribute the yeast evenly throughout the bread. Other companies kneaded the bread by running it through steel rollers.

Rudkin worked hard and she expected the same from her employees. In return, they were paid a little more than the average wages of the time. Other benefits included medical care and insurance. Most of Rudkin's employees were women, and one requirement was that they had no experience in baking bread. Rudkin wanted to teach them to do it her way.

In time, Pepperidge Farm became a family business. Henry Rudkin resigned from his position as a stockbroker in 1949 and went to work full-time for the company. Later, two of the Rudkins' three sons also joined the business. Their other son was more interested in the theater.

By 1951 the Norwalk factory was producing 44,000 loaves a day. They shipped bread to forty-four states and four foreign countries. Gradually, new products were added including a stuffing mix and rolls. In 1956, Rudkin added a line of cookies, and two years later, the company began producing frozen pastries. In 1961, Rudkin sold the business to the Campbell Soup Company for $28 million. However, she continued to serve on the board of directors until her death in 1967.

At one time Rudkin had the distinction of being the only woman to speak at the Harvard School of Business Administration three different times. "I told them the story of the business and how it had succeeded because it had never been run according to any of the accepted rules of manufacturing," she said.[6]

Today, the health benefits of whole wheat bread are well known, but in 1937, homemade whole wheat bread seemed like an old-fashioned idea. That did not stop Rudkin, who with imagination and hard work created a thriving business.

4

Ray Kroc

The Man Behind the Golden Arches

Ray Kroc was fifty-two years old when he opened his first McDonald's Restaurant. The business grew rapidly and people called him an overnight success. Kroc did not agree. He said his previous work as a salesman had prepared him well for his role at McDonald's. "I was just like a lot of show business personalities who work away quietly at the craft for years, and then, suddenly, they get the right break and make it big. I was an overnight success all right, but thirty years is a long, long night."[1]

Raymond Albert Kroc was born in the Chicago suburb of Oak Park, Illinois, on October 5, 1902. His father, Louis Kroc, was employed at Western Union. Although he had worked his way up in the company,

Ray Kroc

he still struggled to make ends meet. Ray decided at a young age that he wanted more for himself.

Ray's mother, Rose, gave piano lessons to earn extra money. She also taught Ray to play. He had a natural talent for the piano, but he hated to give up time with friends to practice. His friends all teased him when his mother interrupted their baseball games calling, "Raymond! It's time to come in and practice."[2]

Ray attended public schools in Oak Park, Illinois. His father had dropped out of school when he was twelve. His dream was that his son would get at least a high school education. However, Ray dropped out after his second year of high school.

The United States was fighting in World War I at the time. Ray volunteered as an ambulance driver for the Red Cross. He was fifteen years old and lied about his age to get the job. He was sent to Connecticut for training with Red Cross Company A. The war ended just as he was about to be shipped out to France.

Ray returned to Chicago and went back to high school, but he dropped out again after only one semester. That summer, he got a job playing piano with a band in the resort area of Paw Paw Lake, Michigan. That was where he met a young woman named Ethel Fleming. They dated for the next three years, while Kroc worked as a musician with bands and orchestras.

Kroc enjoyed the music business, but he did not like the hours—working nights and sleeping days. In 1922, he got a job selling paper cups for the Lily Tulip Cup Company. That same year, he married Ethel Fleming. Kroc was twenty years old. Their daughter, Marilyn, was born in October 1924.

Kroc worked his way up to the position of mid-western sales manager with the Lily Tulip Cup Company. Then in 1937 he started his own small business selling a new invention called the Multimixer. The Multimixer was a machine that could mix five milk shakes at the same time.

By 1954 Multimixer sales had dropped and Kroc was looking for ways to increase business. He became curious about a small drive-in restaurant in San Bernardino, California. The restaurant had bought eight of the machines. It meant that they were set up to mix forty milk shakes at one time. Kroc wondered why anyone would need to make so many milk shakes and he decided to check it out.

On a regular sales trip to California, Kroc took a detour to San Bernardino. He was impressed with what he saw. "They had people standing in line clamoring for those 15-cent hamburgers," he recalled.[3]

When the lunch crowd died down, Kroc visited with the two brothers who owned the restaurant—Richard and Maurice McDonald. They had developed an assembly-line way of preparing food that could be served without a long wait. They were

Ray Kroc demonstrates the Multimixer, a machine that could mix five milk shakes at the same time. His work as a Multimixer salesman led him to Richard and Maurice McDonald and the opportunity for his first McDonald's franchise.

able to do that by featuring a limited menu that centered on hamburgers, French fries, and milk shakes. Another reason that they were able to offer such speedy service was because some of the food was prepared in advance.

Kroc realized that if there were more of this type of restaurant, he would be able to sell more Multimixers. He urged the brothers to open other restaurants, but they were not interested in starting a national chain. Kroc then suggested that he open the restaurants for them.

They made an agreement for Kroc to franchise the restaurants. The company would select sites and build the restaurants. Then they would find franchisees, people to buy the stores. Franchisees bought the right to use the McDonald's trademark and were fully trained in how to run the business. "We give people an opportunity to get into business for themselves, without taking the whole risk alone," Kroc explained. "All we ask is that they follow our way of doing things, the proven way."[4] In return, the owner of each franchise agreed to pay Kroc 1.9 percent of the sales of the restaurant. Out of that 1.9 percent, Kroc paid the McDonald brothers 0.5 percent.

Kroc decided that he would be the owner of the first restaurant, which he opened in the Chicago suburb of Des Plaines, Illinois, on April 15, 1955. He made $366.12 in sales that day. Within two weeks sales had doubled. In September, he opened his first franchised restaurant in Fresno, California, and in December, he opened another one in Resada, California.

Kroc's biggest concern about opening a restaurant in Illinois was whether they would be able to stay open during the winter. The first restaurants were drive-ins with no inside seating. That was not a problem in California where the weather was mild, but Kroc wondered what would happen to sales during the winter months. He did not need to be concerned. "What I didn't realize was that there are nice winter days, when the wind isn't howling and the streets are dry. And there are always people out at noon, like salesmen, who are in a hurry, and they want a hamburger and a cup of coffee and some French fries. They can take the food into their car and the car is warm," Kroc noted.[5]

Realizing the potential of the restaurants, Kroc sold his Multimixer company and used the money to invest in more restaurants. By 1960 there were 228 restaurants.

In 1961, Kroc bought out the McDonald brothers for $2.7 million. That year he also opened Hamburger University, a training center in the Chicago suburb of Elk Grove, Illinois. New franchise owners came to the center for a nineteen-day course on how to run a McDonald's Restaurant. Graduates earned a "Bachelor of Hamburgerology" degree with a minor in French fries.

That same year Kroc and his wife were divorced after thirty-nine years of marriage. Kroc's long working hours had put a strain on their marriage almost from the start. Now, Kroc had fallen in love with Joan (Joni) Smith, the wife of one of the McDonald's franchise owners. Kroc wanted them to both get divorces and marry each other. He got his divorce, but Smith decided that she could not leave her husband.

In 1962, Kroc moved to California, where he met Jane Dobbins Green. They were married two weeks after they met and settled in Woodland Hills, California. Kroc later said that he had rushed into the marriage probably because of his disappointment with the way things had turned out with Smith.

In the meantime the business continued to grow. By 1963 McDonald's had sold more than 1 billion hamburgers. That year they opened restaurant number five hundred and introduced a clown named Ronald McDonald. Three years later they opened their first restaurant with inside seating in Huntsville, Alabama.

In 1968, Kroc decided that it was time to turn the running of the company over to someone else. He became chairman of the board for the McDonald's Corporation and Fred L. Turner became president of the company.

Kroc was speaking at an operators' convention in San Diego when he saw Joan Smith for first time in five years. They still had feelings for each other. This time they both got divorces and Smith and Kroc married on March 8, 1969.

Kroc believed that businesses should be civic-minded. As a result, every McDonald's Restaurant has a community involvement program. These vary with each restaurant, but a popular program is the Ronald McDonald House. This program provides a place for families of seriously ill children to stay while the children are getting treatment at nearby hospitals. Kroc contributed to charities through the Ray Kroc Foundation, which he founded in 1969.

Kroc died of heart failure on January 14, 1984. He was eighty-one years old, but he had never stopped working. He still went to his San Diego office almost every day. With the start of the new millennium in 2000, there were more than 26,000 McDonald's Restaurants in 119 countries. Altogether they served about 43 million people a day. Kroc's original restaurant in Des Plaines, Illinois, is now a museum.

"There's almost nothing you can't accomplish if you set your mind to it," Kroc once told a group of graduate students.[6] It was that kind of confidence that led to his own success as the head of the largest food service retailer in the world.

Colonel Harland Sanders

5

Colonel Harland Sanders
His Secret Recipe

In 1953, Colonel Harland Sanders was the owner of a successful restaurant and motel business in Corbin, Kentucky. The town, nestled along the edge of the Appalachian Mountains, brought a steady stream of tourists to the area. They were a large part of his business. That changed when the government announced plans to build a new interstate bypassing the town of Corbin. The new road routed tourists away from Sanders's business. In 1956, he was forced to sell the business for less than half of what it had been worth three years earlier.

The money from the sale went to pay his debts. All he had left was his monthly Social Security checks of $105 and his own special recipe for the chicken that his customers had enjoyed. At the age of sixty-six, Sanders started over again going out on the road to sell his recipe to restaurant owners.

Harland Sanders was born on a farm near Henryville, Indiana, in 1890. His father died when Harland was six and his mother, Margaret, took on two jobs to support her three children. During the day, she peeled tomatoes at a canning factory and at night she sewed at home for customers. It was up to Harland to look after his three-year-old brother and his baby sister. "We didn't have any baby-sitter, but we got along fine," he recalled.[1] While his mother sewed, she directed Harland in how to cook dinner for the family. By the time he was seven, he could prepare whole meals.

Harland was ten when he got his first paying job working on a neighbor's farm. To his embarrassment, he was fired a month later. The farmer said that Harland spent too much time watching squirrels and birds when he should have been working. Harland never forgot his mother's disappointment. The family needed his income. Determined to do better next time, he got a job with another farmer.

Harland's mother remarried when Harland was twelve. His stepfather was not interested in taking on three children. Harland's brother was sent to live with an aunt in Alabama. Harland dropped out of school and went to work on a farm in Greenwood, Indiana. For the next three years, he lived and worked on the farm. At fifteen he went out on his own, becoming a streetcar conductor in New Albany,

Indiana. At sixteen he enlisted in the army and was stationed in Cuba.

Sanders married when he was still a teenager and he and his wife had three children—a son and two daughters. Over the next several years, Sanders worked at a variety of jobs. He was employed as a carriage painter and a railroad fireman. While working for the railroad, he studied law by correspondence earning a doctor of law degree from Southern University. With that degree, he was able to work as a justice of the peace in Little Rock, Arkansas. Other jobs included working as an insurance salesman and a tire salesman. In 1930, Sanders moved to Corbin, Kentucky, where he opened a gas station. The family lived in quarters at the back of the station.

Sanders got the idea of serving food to the station's customers after a truck driver complained that there were no good places to eat. Sanders served his first customers at the family's dining room table. When the business got too big for the station, Sanders moved into the building across the street. He also decided that it was time for him to get some formal training. "I finally hightailed it up to Cornell University [in New York] and took an eight-week course in Restaurant and Hotel Management, learnin' all about table d-hote and things like how many potatoes to cook."[2]

During this time, he also experimented with seasonings to enhance the taste of the chicken he

Customers wait to be served at the Sanders Café, Colonel Sanders's first restaurant, in Corbin, Kentucky. Sanders was forced to sell the restaurant when a new interstate bypassed the town routing tourists away from his business.

served. By 1935 Sanders was so well known for his fried chicken, that Kentucky Governor Ruby Laffoon gave him the honorary title "Colonel." The governor said the title was for "his contributions to the state's cuisine."[3]

A problem for Sanders was how to prepare the chicken fast enough. If he cooked the chicken when it was ordered, it meant a half-hour wait for the customers. If he cooked it in advance, the chicken would not be fresh.

His problem was solved with the invention of the pressure cooker. The pressure cooker was designed to keep steam inside the pot. This allowed the inside of the cooker to become very hot in a short amount of time. Sanders bought his first pressure cooker in 1939. He experimented until he could cook his chicken just the way he wanted it in about nine minutes.

In 1941, the United States entered World War II. Sanders's business suffered because of gas rationing. In an effort to conserve gas for the war effort, the government limited the amount of gas that citizens could buy. It meant that people were not as free to travel as they had been in the past. After the war business improved again and Sanders added a motel and expanded the restaurant.

While his business grew, his marriage suffered. In 1947, Sanders and his wife were divorced after thirty-nine years of marriage. Two years later Sanders married Claudia Price, a longtime employee of the restaurant.

Sanders made his first attempt at franchising in 1952. It was a simple arrangement. Sanders taught his chicken-cooking process to a friend in Salt Lake City. His friend then agreed to pay Sanders four cents for every chicken he sold. Sanders later made the same arrangement with a few other restaurant owners.

Four years later, when Sanders had to sell his business, he decided to try selling his recipe to other restaurant owners. He loaded his pressure cooker and his mix of flour and special seasonings into his 1946 Ford and set off traveling through Ohio and Indiana.

At that time Sanders was selling his recipe to restaurants that were already up and running. His chicken became part of their menu. He called on restaurant owners offering to cook for them and their staff. "If you like the way it tastes, I'll sell you my seasoning, teach you how to cook it, and you pay me a four-cent royalty on every chicken you sell," Sanders said.[4]

Business was slow. After two years Sanders had signed only five franchise agreements. "When you tell a restaurant man his chicken isn't as good as it ought to be, it usually insults him," Sanders explained.[5] He continued traveling, sometimes sleeping in the backseat of his car to save money. His persistence finally paid off. By 1960 he had agreements with more than two hundred restaurants.

In the early days of the business, Sanders's wife mixed up the ingredients at home and sent them to the restaurants. As the number of restaurants grew, it became necessary to find a manufacturing company to fill the orders. To assure that his recipe of eleven herbs and spices was kept secret, Sanders used two different manufacturers. One manufacturer put together part of the recipe and another one put together the rest. Neither company knew what ingredients the other one used. Sanders never revealed anything about the ingredients except to say that "they stand on everybody's shelf."[6]

By 1963 there were over six hundred outlets, and the business was getting too big for Sanders. "The popularity of Kentucky Fried Chicken was beginning to run right over me and mash me flat," he said.[7] In January 1964, he sold the company for $2 million to a group of investors. The new owners offered Sanders an annual salary to stay on as spokesperson for the company. One of the conditions of the sale was that the investors would not change the Colonel's recipe.

Sanders retained ownership of Kentucky Fried Chicken of Canada. The profits went to the Harland Sanders Foundation. Through that organization, money was donated to charities that included churches, hospitals, the Salvation Army, and the Boy Scouts.

As spokesperson for Kentucky Fried Chicken, Sanders became one of the most familiar faces in the country, traveling over two hundred thousand miles a year. He rode in parades, signed autographs, and spoke to thousands of people. He was in the company's advertisements, appeared on talk shows, and even had small roles in several movies. For all his appearances he dressed in a southern gentleman's attire. It included a white suit, white shirt, and a black string tie. He was an impressive figure dressed in white with his snowy white hair, mustache, and goatee. Sanders owned twenty-five of the white suits and wore out six of them a year.

He continued to be active in promoting the company until he was diagnosed with leukemia in June 1980. He died six months later. At that time Kentucky Fried Chicken had six thousand outlets in forty-eight countries and was still growing. In 1991, the company became known as KFC instead of Kentucky Fried Chicken. The new name better represented the variety of chicken products that KFC now offered.

Today Colonel Sanders's face is again a familiar one. The company launched a new advertising campaign in 1998. It featured an animated character inspired by the face and dress of the Colonel. There are now more than ten thousand KFC restaurants throughout the world, and the Colonel's special recipe remains a well-kept secret.

6

Dave Thomas

Giving Wendy's Customers What They Want

Dave Thomas knows what people want from a family restaurant. "You want to get your money's worth; you want to be treated nice; and it's got to taste good," he said.[1] Giving customers what they wanted made Thomas a millionaire by the time he was thirty-five, but he was just beginning. He had yet to launch the Wendy's Restaurants that have brought him his greatest success.

R. David Thomas was born on July 2, 1932, in Atlantic City, New Jersey. His parents, who were not married, put him up for adoption at birth. Rex and Auleva Thomas of Kalamazoo, Michigan, adopted Dave when he was six weeks old. Auleva Thomas died when Dave was five, leaving only Dave and his father.

Dave Thomas

Dave's father remarried seven months later. That marriage ended in divorce after two and a half years. Dave and his father were on their own again. Dave's father was a construction worker and the two of them moved often as Rex Thomas changed jobs. Dave was lonely and found it hard to make friends. "I never really had a chance to get to know anyone, and I never felt I belonged," he recalled.[2]

Some of the happiest times Dave remembers were when he spent summers with his grandmother, Auleva Thomas's mother, in Augusta, Michigan. His grandmother worked in a restaurant, which sparked an early interest in the food business for Dave. When he traveled with his father, they ate most of their meals in restaurants. Dave paid attention to things like the menu, the atmosphere, and the customers' complaints. "By the age of nine I had become a real expert in restaurants," he said.[3]

Dave's father remarried when Dave was about ten. His stepmother had two daughters from a previous marriage. After living alone with his father, it was hard for Dave to adjust to his new family. Once again, he felt like an outsider.

The family moved to Knoxville, Tennessee, when Dave was twelve. There he got a job delivering groceries. He was fired from that job after a misunderstanding with his boss about vacation time. He then got a job working behind the soda fountain in a drugstore. He was fired from that job when his boss discovered that Dave had lied about his age. He had told the owner that he was sixteen, the legal working age. Dave got another job in a small restaurant in Knoxville. The restaurant owner later said that he suspected that Dave was not sixteen. But the owner decided to overlook Dave's lie because he was such a hard worker.

Dave was only fifteen when he struck out on his own. The family was living in Fort Wayne, Indiana, at the time. Dave was a high school sophomore and was working as a busboy at the Hobby House Restaurant. When his dad said that it was time to move again, Dave decided to stay put. He moved into the local YMCA and continued to work at the restaurant.

He worked the night shift, getting off work at three or four in the morning. He had only a few hours of sleep before he had to go to school. He was not able to keep up that pace for long and soon dropped out of school.

When Thomas turned eighteen, he enlisted in the Army. As part of his training, he enrolled in an eight-week course at Cook and Baker's School. He was then sent to Germany where he worked as a cook in the mess hall. He helped cook meals for about two thousand soldiers a day.

He was later hired as an assistant at the Enlisted Men's Club. Even then, he showed signs of the business instincts that would make him successful in the restaurant business. Thomas realized that the soldiers did not eat at the club because they did not like what was offered. He added fried chicken and hamburgers to the menu and profits increased. "We were doing $40 in food sales when I started, and we ended up grossing $700 a day by the time I left," he recalled.[4]

After his term in the Army, he went back to the Hobby House Restaurant, where he worked as a cook. In 1954, he married Lorraine Buskirk, who was a server at the restaurant.

Thomas met Colonel Sanders of Kentucky Fried Chicken when Thomas's boss bought a Kentucky Fried Chicken franchise in 1956. Thomas got an opportunity to buy into the Kentucky Fried Chicken franchise himself in 1962 when he bought four failing stores in Columbus, Ohio. It was a huge risk buying stores that were not doing well. Colonel Sanders himself advised Thomas against the purchase. Added to Thomas's worries was the fact that he had a growing family to feed. He and his wife already had three daughters and a son. (Another daughter was born later.) But Thomas wanted to be in business for himself.

Thomas took several steps to make those stores more profitable. The first was the most unpleasant. He fired the managers of the stores and brought in more experienced managers. He then gave each of the stores a fresh coat of paint. "Sprucing the places up, I figured, would be good for the employees as well as the customers," he explained.[5]

Next, he focused on advertising. He did not have money for advertising, so he made deals. An example

Dave Thomas in an advertisement for Wendy's Restaurants. Thomas has enjoyed success as spokesperson for the company he founded. People like his folksy image.

was a deal he made with a radio station manager. Thomas traded him chicken for ads.

Thomas turned those stores around, and in 1968, he sold them for $1.5 million. He could have retired, but at thirty-five he was not ready for that. With money from the sale of his Kentucky Fried Chicken stores, he opened his first Wendy's Restaurant in downtown Columbus, Ohio, on November 15, 1969. The restaurant was named after his eight-year-old daughter, Melinda Lou, who went by the nickname Wendy.

Thomas's idea was to offer hamburgers made from fresh meat, rather than the frozen patties popular with other fast food chains. His square-shaped hamburgers were cooked fresh. "People don't make sandwiches at home and put them under a heat lamp," he said. "So we don't."[6]

A year later Thomas opened his second restaurant in Columbus. In June 1972, he opened a restaurant in Indianapolis, the first Wendy's outside of Ohio. By 1982 Wendy's had 2,430 stores. The business was running smoothly and Thomas turned the operation over to a management team.

Unfortunately, by 1989, Wendy's International was in trouble. Sales were down and stores were closing. Thomas asked James Near, a Wendy's franchise owner, to take over. Near agreed, but he had one condition. He wanted Thomas to take an active role in the company again.

Thomas became the spokesperson for the company, appearing in their advertisements. People liked his folksy image and he was at least part of the reason for an increase in profits. Another part of his new role was visiting Wendy's franchises. Thomas spends about thirty-five weeks each year traveling to the restaurants, meeting employees, and checking on quality in those restaurants. "In a franchise company you have to have someone who is inspirational," one franchise owner noted. "Who can do that better than Dave Thomas—the founder?"[7]

In 1990, President George Bush named Thomas national spokesperson for adoption. Two years later Thomas founded the Dave Thomas Foundation for Adoption. The foundation focuses on making adoption easier and more affordable. Profits from two books he has written—*Dave's Way* and *Well Done!*—go to support the foundation. Money he makes from speaking engagements also goes toward adoption programs. He encourages Wendy's employees to adopt by giving them time off and financial help to do so.

Thomas also got involved in a national campaign urging kids to stay in school. One day a teenager challenged Thomas reminding Thomas that he himself did not have a diploma. The youth said that Thomas should set a good example. Thomas took the challenge. He hired a tutor and began studying to take the GED high school equivalency diploma exam. He graduated from the Coconut Creek High

School in Fort Lauderdale, Florida, in 1993. His classmates voted him "Most Likely to Succeed."[8]

One regret for Thomas is that he spent so much time working that he did not have time to be a father. "He was always overtired," one daughter recalled. "He really didn't know how to treat kids, didn't know how to go to a baseball game. My mom really held it [the family] together."[9] However, Thomas does have a good relationship now with his adult children, and they are all involved in the Wendy's business.

In 1996, Thomas suffered a heart attack. His recovery included lifestyle changes which meant losing forty pounds, although he still enjoys eating a Wendy's hamburger. Today, there are more than five thousand Wendy's Restaurants in thirty-two countries. Thomas is still active as the spokesperson for the company.

Thomas believes that success is within anyone's reach. "There's no reason in the world that a dirt-poor kid like me with a jumbled home life who dropped out of school should have made it, but I did—at least in some ways. And if I can, you can. Anybody can," he says.[10]

Wally Amos

Wally Amos

"The Face That Launched a Thousand Chips"

In 1975, Wally Amos founded his Famous Amos Chocolate Chip Cookie Company, becoming the first person to open a retail cookie store. Amos, with his friendly, outgoing personality was a natural at promoting his product. He became a regular on talk shows and radio programs. He referred to himself as "the face that launched a thousand chips."[1] But Amos made mistakes. By 1988 he had lost control of his company and later even lost the right to use his own name in promoting a new cookie business. Still, he refused to be discouraged, and in 1992 he started over again.

Wally Amos was born in Tallahassee, Florida, on July 1, 1936. He was the only child of Ruby and

Wallace Amos, Sr. Wally's father was a laborer and his mother worked as a domestic helper. Although Wally respected his parents, he recalled that they rarely laughed or showed any affection. They were strict in both how they raised their son and in their religious beliefs. "Anything that appeared to be fun, like dancing, was a sin in the Amos home," he noted.[2]

In 1948, when Wally was twelve, his parents separated and later divorced. Wally's mother sent him to live with her sister, Della, in New York City. Life with his Aunt Della and Uncle Fred was very different from Wally's early years in Florida. Aunt Della laughed often and loved to play practical jokes. It was Aunt Della who introduced Wally to the chocolate chip cookie that would later make him famous. "When those cookies came out of the oven I licked the bowl, the spoon, the whole thing. I was in love," he recalled.[3]

A recruiter at Food Trades Vocational High School convinced Wally to attend high school there and study to become a chef. After his second year, Wally decided that he did not want to spend long hours in a hot kitchen. He dropped out of high school and joined the Air Force.

Amos spent four years in the Air Force where he earned his GED high school equivalency diploma. He then returned to New York City and got a job as a stock clerk at Saks Fifth Avenue department store. After five years at Saks, he got a job at the William Morris Agency, a well-known talent agency.

Amos started in the mail room. Within a year, he worked up to the position of talent agent, the first African-American agent in the company's history. The company had started a rock-and-roll division and Amos helped get that branch of the business off the ground. His clients included the Temptations, the Supremes, and Simon and Garfunkel.

In the meantime Amos had married Maria La Forey and they had two sons. That marriage ended in divorce. In 1966, Amos married Shirlee Ellis. Their son, Shawn, was born in September 1967. Shortly after his son's birth, Amos moved his family to the West Coast where he opened his own talent agency in Hollywood. By 1970 Amos's second marriage had ended.

Amos began making chocolate chip cookies as a kind of therapy, to help him relax after a day at work. His cookies became his calling card. He handed them out to clients and served them at meetings with Hollywood executives.

His friends encouraged him to sell the cookies. Amos decided to take that advice after he became dissatisfied with his talent agency. "I got tired of not making any money and constantly giving all my energy to someone else," he explained. "I realized that I could still be in the same situation 10 years from then."[4] It was time to do something he really enjoyed.

With $25,000 borrowed from friends in the entertainment business, Amos launched the Famous

Amos Chocolate Chip Cookie Company. He opened his first cookie store on Sunset Boulevard in Los Angeles on March 10, 1975.

As the owner of his own cookie company, Amos adopted a style of dressing that suited his friendly personality more than a business suit. Dressed in a Panama hat and a Hawaiian print shirt, he took to the street handing out samples of his cookies.

A few months after opening the store, Amos began wholesaling his cookies. It meant that he sold his cookies to stores that in turn, sold the cookies to their customers. Before long, the cookies were being sold in upscale department stores such as Macy's, Bloomingdale's, and Neiman Marcus. The cookies were packaged in a brown bag decorated with Amos's smiling bearded face. The stores also sold Famous Amos T-shirts, jewelry, duffel bags, and umbrellas. By 1977 Amos had two factories produce his cookies. One was in Van Nuys, California, and the other in Nutley, New Jersey. The company was manufacturing six tons of cookies each week.

Amos spent his time promoting his cookies and hired friends to handle the day-to-day operations of the company. In fact, Amos even put physical distance between him and his cookie factories when he moved to Hawaii in 1977. Amos had fallen in love with the state when he went there to promote his cookies. He later opened three stores on the islands.

In July 1979, he married his third wife, Christine Harris. Their daughter, Sarah, was born in 1980.

That year, the Smithsonian Institution honored Amos when they enshrined his Panama hat and his Hawaiian shirt in their advertising section.

Amos soon learned that hiring friends to run the business was not a good idea. "I hired people to run the company who didn't know what they were doing and made mistakes," he noted.[5] In 1985, sales were good, but because of mismanagement, the company was losing money. To raise money to keep the business going, Amos found investors. "The investors put money into the corporation and in return they got stock," Amos explained.[6] The investors took over the running of the company bringing in their own management team.

Over the next few years, investors were bought out by other investors. Then in 1988 the Shansby Group from San Francisco bought the company. They hired Amos as spokesperson for the company. A year later Amos decided that he did not like being an employee of the company he had founded, and he resigned. At that time the new owners had him sign a "non-compete" agreement. According to the terms of that agreement, Amos was prevented from starting a new cookie business for two years.

It was a hard time for Amos. "The first couple of years after I left Famous Amos, I didn't even make cookies anymore, and I used to always make cookies at home. I didn't even want to talk about chocolate chip cookies, really. I shaved my beard and stopped wearing hats," he said.[7]

Amos kept busy giving motivational speeches throughout the country. He also devoted much of his time to charitable organizations. Since 1979 he has been a national spokesperson for Literacy Volunteers of America, an organization that helps adults and teens learn to read. He has also served as a member of the board of directors for a dropout prevention program called Cities in Schools, and as a board member of the National Center for Family Literacy.

In 1991, when his "non-compete" agreement with Famous Amos was up, Amos launched another cookie business, Wally Amos Presents: Chip & Cookie. He closed the business the following year when Famous Amos started a legal battle to prevent him from using his name to promote his cookies. The court ruled in favor of Famous Amos, and Wally Amos was barred from using his own name or the word *famous* to advertise any cookie, food, or beverage companies or restaurant franchises.

On the other hand, Amos was no longer prevented from operating a cookie business. In 1992, he launched the Uncle Noname (pronounced No-NAHM-ay) Cookie Company. Amos hired a professional management team to run the business. He was in charge of promotion. He also continued his charitable work and giving motivational speeches. He is also the author of four autobiographical and inspirational books.

In 1998, the Keebler Company bought Famous Amos. They hired Amos to be a spokesperson for the

Wally Amos wears a hat and shirt designed for his Uncle Noname Cookie Company. Amos chose that name after courts barred him from using his own name.

cookies. Amos agreed, but with one condition. Over the years with the changes in ownership, the recipe for Famous Amos cookies had changed. It was something that Amos realized as soon as he bit into one of the cookies. He said that he could not represent the cookie the way it was. If he was to be the spokesperson, they needed to go back to the original recipe. Keebler agreed.

Today, Wally Amos is once again promoting Famous Amos cookies in appearances at grocery stores and trade shows. "I will always be Famous Amos," he said.[8]

According to the terms of his agreement with Keebler, Amos is also allowed to use his own name for his business. In 1999, Amos launched a new product line—low-fat and fat-free muffins. They are sold under the name Uncle Wally's.

8

Debbi Fields

Serving Cookies Fresh from the Oven

When Debbi Fields said that she wanted to open a store to sell her chocolate chip cookies, she was told that it would not work. "America loves crispy cookies," her friends and her husband's business associates said.[1] Hers were soft and chewy, like cookies fresh from the oven. Yet Fields noticed that the same people who said that her cookies would not sell, were obviously enjoying her cookies. She decided to follow her instincts and on August 18, 1977, she opened her first cookie store. Ten years later, the company had nearly five hundred stores in thirty-seven states and it was still growing.

Debra Jane Sivyer was born in Oakland, California, on September 18, 1956. Her father,

Debbi Fields

Edward, was a World War II veteran who worked as a civilian welder for the Navy. Her mother, Mary, was a full-time homemaker. Debbi, the youngest of five daughters, felt a need to stand out from her sisters, to prove that she was special. Baking cookies was one thing that she did well. By the time she was thirteen, she had already created her recipe for chocolate chip cookies. She had also discovered the secret that would make her a success in the cookie business— the best cookies came from the best ingredients.

As a teenager, she learned the value of hard work. Her family was not poor, but they did not have much money for extras. "I learned early in life that if I wanted to have something, I had to work for it," she said.[2] Her first job was chasing foul balls for the Oakland A's professional baseball team. She was thirteen and the first female the team had hired for that position. When she was fifteen, she began working at a department store after school and on weekends. Two years later, Debbi, who had been water-skiing since she was five years old, got a job as a water-skier at Marine World. She later became a performer in a dolphin show at the park.

Debbi also enjoyed snow skiing. After graduating from high school in 1973, she moved to Lake Tahoe, a ski resort area on the California/Nevada border. She worked as a nanny there and spent her free time skiing the Lake Tahoe slopes. After a few months, she quit that job and moved back to Oakland. She began working at a department store, saving her money to finance ski trips to Utah, Colorado, and Nevada. She also took classes at Los Altos Community College.

One day, when she was stranded by bad weather at an airport in Utah, a man walked up and introduced himself as Randy Fields. He was twenty-eight years old, ten years older than Debbi was. He already had a successful career as a financial consultant. His job was to predict business trends. He, too, was from California and shared her interest in skiing. In spite of their age difference, they fell in love and were married on September 21, 1976. Debbi Fields had just celebrated her twentieth birthday.

As a young newlywed, Fields often felt uncomfortable around her husband's older, well-educated friends.[3] Her husband was busy with his work, and she longed to have work of her own. She often baked cookies for her husband's business associates, who praised her abilities. That was what gave her the idea to open a store where she could sell her cookies.

Unfortunately, Fields discovered that others were not as enthusiastic about her plan as she was. "People thought I was crazy to even consider going into business, let alone a cookie business," she recalled.[4]

Several banks turned down her request for a loan, but she kept trying. She finally found a banker who would loan her $50,000 to start up her business, but only if her husband cosigned the loan. As cosigner, Randy Fields agreed that if his wife was not able to pay back the loan, he would. The money went to purchasing commercial baking equipment, which

Fields bought used. She also found a store to rent in a food arcade in Palo Alto, California. On August 18, 1977, Mrs. Fields Chocolate Chippery opened for business. (The name was later changed to Mrs. Fields, Inc. to reflect a wider range of products.)

On her first day of business, Fields got to the store at 6:00 A.M. She baked until opening time at 9:00 A.M. Then she waited. By noon she had not sold a single cookie. Fields took a tray of cookies and walked out into the mall giving out samples. "I thought I made the best chocolate chip cookies, and I wanted to get one in everybody's mouth," she said.[5] Her strategy worked. By the end of the day she had made $50.

Sales steadily increased and Fields soon hired her first employee, a woman to manage the store when Fields was not there. Fields liked to have fun at work and she looked for employees with the same attitude. "I hired people on the basis of warmth, friendliness, and ability to have a good time, and together we became a team," she explained.[6]

A few months after Fields opened her store, the owner of Pier 39, a new shopping mall in San Francisco, asked Fields to open another store in his mall. It was a big decision for Fields, who had never thought beyond that first store. She took eight months to think about it before opening a store in the mall in 1979. That same year, her daughter, Jessica, was born.

With the Pier 39 store up and running, Fields began actively looking to open new stores. She decided against franchising because she did not think that she would be able to control quality. A quality product was Fields's first priority. If the cookies were not just right, Fields was known to throw out the whole batch. The cookies also had to be fresh. Any that weren't sold within two hours were given to charitable organizations.

In 1981, Fields's daughter, Jenessa, was born. That year Fields moved the company headquarters to Park City, Utah. The company was operating fourteen stores at the time, and that number was growing rapidly.

By 1984 the company was operating 160 stores with locations in 17 states and four foreign cities— Hong Kong, Tokyo, Singapore, and Sydney. Randy Fields had joined the company as chief financial officer. However, the gourmet cookie business was getting crowded, and Randy and Debbi Fields decided that the company needed to branch out into other areas. In 1987, they bought La Petite Boulangerie, a French bakery/sandwich shop chain. The cost of buying the stores and getting them running was more than they expected. In 1988, the company suffered a $19 million loss and had to close about ninety stores.

It was obvious to Fields that she needed to make changes. The company was growing quickly and she was trying to do too much of the work herself. That year she put together a team of professional managers, and removed herself from some of the day-to-day operations of the business. It meant a new way of thinking for Fields. "[In the past] if I saw something I didn't like, I fixed it myself, right then and there," Fields said. "Those days are over. Now I literally have to stop myself. Letting go has been hard."[7]

On the other hand, that change gave her time to focus on planning for future growth of the company. It also gave her more time to spend with her growing family, which included three more daughters. Jennifer was born in 1984, Ashley in 1988, and McKenzie in 1991.

Unfortunately, the company's financial problems continued into the 1990s, which brought about more changes. In 1990, the company instituted a franchising system, which allowed store managers to buy their stores if the managers met certain goals. Three years later, faced with a $94 million debt, Fields was forced to surrender 80 percent of the company to its lenders. She remained the company's largest individual stockholder with 11 percent of the stock. She also served on the company's board of directors, but she gave up her position as president of the company. "I had to be responsible, to make sure everyone would get paid, so I became an insignificant shareholder. It was very difficult, but it allowed me to grow in a dimension I otherwise never would have," she explained.[8]

Debbi Fields tastes one of her soft, chewy chocolate chip cookies. Fields' priority was a quality product. She was known to throw out a whole batch of cookies if they were not just right.

Fields focused on areas that she enjoyed most—public relations and new product development, which included creating her own recipes. Fields is the author of four cookbooks of her original dessert recipes. She also branched out into other areas such as hosting a daily cable television program, *The Dessert Show.*

Today the company has over 650 locations in the United States and operates 65 locations in 11 different countries. Fields gave up her position on the board of directors, one of several recent changes in her life. In 1997, she and Randy Fields divorced. A year later, she married Michael Rose, a retired hotel executive. She now makes her home in Memphis, Tennessee.

Fields is a popular public speaker describing how a young housewife with no business experience built a $150 million business. "The important thing is not being afraid to take a chance," she has said. "Remember, the greatest failure is to not try."[9]

Ben Cohen (left) and Jerry Greenfield

9

Ben Cohen and Jerry Greenfield
The Ice Cream Guys

Ben Cohen and Jerry Greenfield wanted a business that was different from the large corporations that appeared to be all about profit. With their business, they would focus on making people happy rather than just getting rich. They also wanted it to be a fun place to work. "If it isn't fun, why do it?" Greenfield said.[1] That became their company motto when they opened their Ben & Jerry's Homemade ice cream scoop shop on May 5, 1978.

Bennett Cohen and Jerry Greenfield were born just four days apart in Brooklyn, New York, in March 1951. They both attended public schools in Merrick, Long Island, but did not meet until they ended up in the same seventh grade gym class. "We

83

were the two slowest, chubbiest guys in the seventh grade," Greenfield recalled. "We were nerds."[2]

The first time Jerry saw Ben was when the class was running a mile on the track. Ben and Jerry were lagging way behind. The gym teacher hollered at them telling them that if they could not run the mile in seven minutes, they would have to do it over again. That made no sense to Ben who argued, "But, Coach, if we can't do it in less than seven minutes the first time, how are we gonna do it in under seven minutes the second time?"[3] The way Ben spoke up impressed Jerry. He knew right away that Ben was someone he wanted as a friend.

They both graduated from Calhoun High School in Merrick. Greenfield, enrolled at Oberlin College in Oberlin, Ohio, where he studied premed. After graduating from Oberlin College, Greenfield applied to medical schools but was turned down. He moved to New York City, where he worked as a lab technician.

Cohen enrolled at Colgate University in Hamilton, New York. He dropped out after a year and a half. For a while he attended Skidmore College in Saratoga Springs, New York, where he studied pottery and jewelry making. In the meantime he worked at a variety of jobs. He was a cashier at McDonald's, a security guard, a manager at an apartment complex, and a cab driver in New York City. He also worked as a craft teacher at a residential school for emotionally disturbed children.

By 1977 the friends decided to start their own business. The next decision was to figure out what type of business it would be. "Since we love to eat, we immediately thought of food," Greenfield joked.[4]

They considered making bagels, but gave up that idea when they found out that the equipment was too expensive. Their next choice was ice cream. They split the cost of a $5 correspondence class on ice cream making, and then began creating their own flavors. They wanted to live in a small college town, so they opened their business in Burlington, Vermont, the home of the University of Vermont. With $12,000 ($4,000 of it borrowed), they converted an old gas station into an ice cream shop.

Cohen, who was in charge of marketing, did not advertise in the usual way. His advertising was mainly in the form of events. To get more customers into the store that first summer, they hosted free outdoor movie festivals. They used the side of the store next door as a screen for the movies they showed.

Sales were good, but the partners knew that business would drop off during the winter. Unfortunately, their bills would continue to come. They needed to find another market for their ice cream. In January 1979, they began wholesaling their ice cream, selling it to restaurants by the gallon.

They celebrated their first-year anniversary in business with a Free Cone Day. It was their way of showing appreciation for their customers. "Early on," Greenfield said, "we knew that if we stayed in the business, it was because of the support of a lot of people, so it seemed natural to want to return that support."[5]

In February 1980, the partners expanded their wholesale business. They began packing their ice cream in pint containers to market in grocery stores. To make room for their wholesale business, they rented space in an old spool and bobbin mill.

A year later they moved again into a larger building for their growing operation. In addition to sales to grocery stores and restaurants, the partners wanted to franchise stores like their scoop shop in Burlington. That year, they opened their first franchise store in Shelburne, Vermont.

As the business grew, the financial end of it became too much for the partners. One day they actually closed the store just to pay bills and try to make some sense out of their financial records. Even worse, they feared that they were becoming what they did not want to be—businessmen concerned about profits and losses. Their first impulse was to sell the business. In fact, Greenfield did take some time off noting that the business had become "too big" for him. "I was more comfortable in the filling station," he said.[6]

Greenfield's girlfriend, later his wife, moved to Arizona to work on a Ph.D. degree, and Greenfield went with her. He stayed involved with the business returning a few times a year to help Cohen with special events. He also retained part ownership in the company. Cohen continued on with the company with the help of a general manager hired to handle the financial end of the business.

As demand for their ice cream increased, a larger factory was needed. To raise money for the factory, the partners decided to sell stock in the company. It gave people an opportunity to own part of the company by buying shares. Taking advantage of a little known-legal clause, the first shares were offered to Vermont residents only.

In 1985, they moved into the new factory built in Waterbury, Vermont. That year Greenfield came back from Arizona and began taking a daily role in the company again. Although Cohen and Greenfield feared too much growth, they now felt a responsibility to their stockholders who expected to make money from their investment. They decided that maybe profit was not such a bad thing. What was more important was what they did with their earnings.

They had been donating to charities informally, giving about 5 percent of the company's before-tax profits. In 1985, they made a more formal arrangement for charitable giving by founding the Ben & Jerry's Foundation. Through the Foundation, the company would donate 7.5 percent of the company's before-tax profits to charitable programs throughout the United States. (Most companies give about 1–1.5 percent). Contributions have gone to programs to support children's rights, the homeless, and the environment.

They also looked for additional ways to help others. One thing they did was develop different flavors of ice cream to help various groups. For example, the brownies used in their Chocolate Fudge Brownie ice cream were baked by unemployed and homeless people in Yonkers, New York. The blueberries in their Wild Maine Blueberry ice cream was made with blueberries harvested by the Passamaquoddy Indians.

Greenfield and Cohen also wanted happy employees. "I want our people to love their work and have positive feelings about the company," Cohen said.[7] One way to accomplish that was with good benefits. Along with traditional medical and dental benefits, Ben & Jerry's offered affordable day care, help with college tuition, and free health-club memberships. An unusual benefit was that each employee was allowed to take home three free pints of ice cream each day.

The partners also encouraged an open exchange of ideas between employees and managers. In most companies, supervisors evaluate the work performance of their employees. At Ben & Jerry's, employees were also allowed to evaluate their supervisors. Production was shut down so that all employees could attend monthly staff meetings. These meetings gave them a chance to voice their opinions about work. They could also vote on what charities they thought the company should support.

Often in businesses, people in the top positions earn large salaries, while those in entry-level positions earn very little in comparison. The partners did not want to see that happen at Ben & Jerry's, so they set up a five-to-one salary ratio. According to this plan, no one in the company could make more than five times the salary of someone in the lowest-paying position.

In 1988, Greenfield founded the Joy Gang. Employees took turns serving on a committee whose only purpose was to make work more fun. Activities planned by the committee included employees giving massages to other employees, Halloween parties, and an "Elvis Appreciation Day." On that day, everyone was encouraged to come to work dressed like rock-and-roll singer Elvis Presley.

By 1991 the company had ninety franchise shops nationwide and had opened a second factory in Springfield, Vermont. That year they introduced a new flavor called Chocolate Chip Cookie Dough, which quickly became its most popular flavor. They also introduced a new line of Low Fat Frozen Yogurt.

As the company grew, Cohen and Greenfield had to make hard compromises. One compromise was changes to the five-to-one salary ratio. The ratio made it hard for them to hire people to fill management positions. Other companies were paying much more for their top executives. To attract executives to the company, the ratio had to be changed to

Jerry Greenfield (left) and Ben Cohen serve up free cones in honor of the 20th anniversary of their company in 1998. They had also celebrated their first anniversary with a Free Cone Day as a way of showing appreciation for their customers.

seven-to-one. Eventually, the partners were forced to abandon it altogether.

In 1994, the company was earning $150 million a year. They had six hundred employees and were operating three manufacturing plants. That year Cohen announced his plans to step down as CEO (Chief Executive Officer). He said that it was time to turn the management over to people who were better trained. The partners still remained active in the company. They focused on the things they liked to do best—developing new flavors and working on long-term planning and customer relations. But perhaps this change in roles was a sign of things to come. In April 2000, the partners sold the company for $326 million to the Unilever corporation.

Although the partners were reluctant to sell, pressure from stockholders convinced them that it was the right thing to do. For its part, Unilever assured the partners that the charitable giving that they had begun would continue under the new leadership.

Ben & Jerry's has become a model for other companies who have made charitable giving a part of their business policy. Ben & Jerry's ice cream is still found in grocery freezers. Flavors with fun-sounding names such as Chunky Monkey, Chubby Hubby, and Jerry's Jubilee are a reminder of the two regular guys who created a different kind of company.

Paul Newman

Paul Newman

The Company Founded for Charities

Actor Paul Newman has starred in over sixty films in a career that has spanned more than fifty years. But acting is only one of his talents. He is also a director and a race car driver. In 1982, he became a businessman when he and a partner founded Newman's Own, a company whose entire after-tax profits go to charity.

Paul Leonard Newman was born in Cleveland, Ohio, on January 26, 1925. He was the younger of Arthur and Theresa Newman's two children. His brother, Arthur Newman Jr., was a year older than him.

Arthur Newman, Sr. and his brother were partners in a successful sporting goods store. The family lived comfortably in Shaker Heights, an upscale

Cleveland suburb. Paul attended Shaker Heights High School, graduating in 1943. The United States was fighting in World War II then, and Newman enlisted in the Navy. He served as a radio operator during the war, flying in the backseat of torpedo bombers over the South Pacific.

He received his honorable discharge from the Navy in 1946 and enrolled at Kenyon College in Gambier, Ohio. Newman played on the college football team and ran a campus laundry to earn extra money. He got interested in acting after he was kicked off the football team because of a fight in a local nightclub. Over the next two years, he performed in ten college productions.

He graduated in 1949 and that same day he left for Williams Bay, Wisconsin, to work in a summer theater. There he met and fell in love with fellow actor Jacqueline Witte. When the summer season ended, Newman signed on with the Woodstock Players, a theater company near Chicago.

Newman and Witte were married in December 1949. A few months later, in May 1950, Newman's father died. Newman returned to Cleveland to work in the family business. Later that year Newman and his wife celebrated the birth of their son, Scott.

Newman lasted only a year in retail. In 1951, he and his wife and son moved to New Haven, Connecticut. Newman enrolled at Yale University School of Drama to study for a master's degree in directing. At that time he was not thinking about an acting career. "I was running away from the sporting goods business," he recalled.[1]

Newman did so well acting in his first year at Yale, that some of his instructors encouraged him to try his luck in New York during the summer. In June 1952, he moved his family to New York City and started looking for work as an actor.

He quickly landed a couple of television appearances and a small continuing role on a series called *The Aldrich Family*. In 1953, he made his Broadway debut in a play called *Picnic*. Newman launched his movie career with *The Silver Chalice*, which premiered in 1954. "It was probably the worst film ever done," Newman later said.[2] Fortunately, better roles followed.

In addition to their son, Newman and his wife, Jacqueline, had two daughters, Susan and Stephanie, before their marriage ended in divorce in 1957. On January 29, 1958, Newman married actress Joanne Woodward. They had first met in 1953 when they were both appearing in *Picnic*. Over the next few years, Newman and Woodward had three daughters—Nell, Melissa, and Cleo. Newman wanted his children to have a normal life away from Hollywood, so they settled in Westport, Connecticut.

Newman attended racing school when he was preparing for his role as a race car driver for the movie *Winning*, released in 1968. He enjoyed the experience so much that he began racing in amateur events, a hobby he has continued for more than thirty years.

By 1982 Newman had made forty-eight movies and was looking for other interests to pursue. That's when he and his friend, author A. E. Hotchner, launched the Newman's Own food company. Newman's homemade vinegar, oil, and herb salad dressing had long been a family favorite. For years, Newman and Hotchner had been bottling the salad dressing in wine bottles to give to their friends as Christmas presents. In 1982, they decided to sell a few bottles commercially and give the money to charity.

They had planned to market the salad dressing only on the East Coast, but within six months they were selling it nationwide. During their first year of business, they gave away nearly $1 million to charity.

Other products were added including additional varieties of salad dressing, spaghetti sauce, lemonade, popcorn, and steak sauce. Newman also made an arrangement with Ben & Jerry's to have them create special ice cream flavors to be sold as Newman's Own ice cream.

Newman takes pleasure in writing the humorous stories that appear on Newman's Own products. An example is the paragraph about Butch Cassidy on the back of Newman's Own ranch dressing. Newman played outlaw Butch Cassidy in the popular 1969 movie, *Butch Cassidy and the Sundance Kid*. According to the story Newman wrote, the recipe for the ranch dressing was one of the few things found in Butch Cassidy's pocket at the time of his death. On the back of the recipe Cassidy had written: "this stuff is so good it ought to be outlawed."[3]

Newman originally objected to the idea of having his face imprinted on the product packages, but he decided to go ahead with it if it would help sales. Certainly, Newman's success as an actor has boosted sales. On the other hand, Newman occasionally gets mail from people who do not know about his acting career. A man who liked Newman's spaghetti sauce wrote: "My girlfriend mentioned that you were a movie star and I would be interested to know what you've made. If you act as well as you cook, your movies would be worth watching."[4] Newman hung the letter on his office wall.

The company has donated to hundreds of charities including groups for the homeless and mentally retarded. They have purchased buses for migrant workers in Florida and assisted victims of natural disasters all around the world. They have also given money to the Scott Newman Foundation. Newman and Woodward created this organization after Newman's son, Scott, died from an accidental drug overdose in 1978. The purpose of the foundation is to create drug education films and programs.

Another charity close to Newman's heart is his Hole in the Wall Gang Camp. This summer camp for children with life-threatening illnesses opened in 1988. Newman got the idea for the camp after two

Paul Newman has always been interested in doing good things. Here he is at the March on Washington, D.C. in 1963. Dr. Martin Luther King, Jr. and other civil rights leaders had organized a massive march. It was intended to highlight African-American unemployment and to urge Congress to pass a wide-ranging civil rights bill.

of his friends died of cancer. His friends were adults, but it made Newman think about all the children with cancer. "After they [his friends] died, I found myself thinking, Well, at least they had some opportunities. What about the kids who are facing a short life or one in which their experiences will be extremely limited?"[5] Newman wanted to do something to give those children a chance to forget about their illness for a while.

The camp is located near Ashford, Connecticut. According to a report in *Reader's Digest*, it cost $17 million to build. Newman's Own donated $8 million. The rest came from other contributors, including a $5 million gift from a twenty-five year old Saudi Arabian businessman. He had suffered from a blood disorder ever since childhood.

The name of the camp comes from the movie *Butch Cassidy and the Sundance Kid*. The Hole in the Wall Gang was the name of their gang of outlaws. The camp is designed to look like a frontier town in the early 1900s. The children stay in log cabins. There is a lake for fishing and there are hiking trails, horses, and other animals. There is even a cave representing the hideout of the Hole in the Wall Gang. Although the camp has a complete medical staff to meet the special needs of the children, Newman wanted nothing in the camp to remind the children of a hospital. Newman is a frequent visitor at the camp, often joining the children in their activities.

Although Newman's Own started the camp, it now operates on private donations. There are currently six camps for children with serious illnesses, including camps in Florida, New York, Illinois, and the countries of Ireland and France.

In November 1999, Newman's Own reached a milestone surpassing the $100 million mark in donations to charity. "The embarrassing thing," Newman has joked, "is that the salad dressing is out-grossing my films."[6]

There is now also a second generation of Newman's Own started by Newman's daughter, Nell. She sells organic products including pretzels, chocolate bars, tortilla chips, and Fig Newmans.

Newman still takes pleasure in personally selecting charities for donations. "I'm not a professional philanthropist, and I'm not running for sainthood. I just happen to think that in life we need to be a little like the farmer who puts back into the soil what he takes out," Newman said.[7] Newman's Own is his way of giving back to all the fans who have supported his acting career.

Chapter Notes

Preface

1. Mike Capuzzo, "When the Chips Are Down, Amos Fights," *Houston Chronicle*, September 7, 1994, p. 3.

2. Sandy Naiman, "Debbi Fields Is One Smart Cookie," *Toronto Sun*, January 18, 1999, <http://www.slam.ca/CNEWSLifeArchive/990118_cookie.html> (August 23, 2001).

Chapter 1. Milton S. Hershey

1. Timothy M. Erdman, "Hershey: Sweet Smell of Success," *American History Illustrated*, March/April 1994, p. 65.

2. Roy Bongartz, "The Chocolate Camelot," *American Heritage*, June 1973, p. 7.

3. James C. Young, "Hershey, Unique Philanthropist," *The New York Times*, November 18, 1923, section 9: Special Features, p. 4.

4. Ibid.

5. Bongartz, p. 95.

Chapter 2. W. K. Kellogg

1. *"I'll Invest My Money in People,"* Battle Creek, Mich.: W. K. Kellogg Foundation, 1998, p. 45.

2. W. Guzzardi, "The U.S. Business Hall of Fame," *Fortune*, March 13, 1989, p. 135.

3. *"I'll Invest My Money in People,"* p. 32.

4. Horace B. Powell, *The Original Has This Signature— W. K. Kellogg* (Englewood Cliffs, N.J.: Prentice-Hall, Inc., 1956), p. 59.

5. Joseph J. Fucini and Suzy Fucini, *Entrepreneurs: The Men and Women Behind Famous Brand Names and How They Made It* (Boston: G.K. Hall & Co., 1985), p. 155.

The Founders of Famous Food Companies

6. Ibid., p. 157.

7. *"I'll Invest My Money in People,"* p. 50.

Chapter 3. Margaret Rudkin

1. Margaret Rudkin, *The First Twenty-Five Years* (Norwalk, Conn.: Pepperidge Farm, Inc., 1962), p. 4.

2. Ibid.

3. John Bainbridge, "Profiles: Striking a Blow for Grandma," *The New Yorker*, May 22, 1948, p. 40.

4. Rudkin, p. 5.

5. J. D. Ratcliff, "Bread, de Luxe," *Reader's Digest*, December 1939, p. 102.

6. Bainbridge, p. 42.

Chapter 4. Ray Kroc

1. Ray Kroc, *Grinding It Out: The Making of McDonald's* (Chicago: Saint Martin's Press, LLC, 1977), p. 101.

2. Ibid., p. 16.

3. J. Anthony Lukas, "As American as a McDonald's Hamburger on the Fourth of July," *The New York Times Magazine*, July 4, 1971, p. 22.

4. Ibid.

5. "Lessons of Leadership: Part XXXVIII—Appealing to a Mass Market," *Nation's Business*, July 1968, p. 74.

6. Kroc, p. 59.

Chapter 5. Colonel Harland Sanders

1. William Whitworth, "Profiles: Kentucky-Fried," *New Yorker*, February 14, 1970, p. 41.

2. Jodi Lawrence, "Chicken Big and the Citizen Senior," *The Washington Post, Potomac Magazine*, November 9, 1969, p. 40.

3. James Stewart-Gordon, "Saga of the 'Chicken' Colonel," *Reader's Digest*, February 1975, p. 144.

4. Ibid., p. 145.

5. "Chicken Colonel," *Newsweek*, July 25, 1966, p. 79.

102

6. Edith Evans Asbury, "Col. Harland Sanders, Founder of Kentucky Fried Chicken, Dies," *The New York Times*, December 17, 1980, p. A33.

7. "Chicken Colonel," p. 79.

Chapter 6. Dave Thomas

1. *Dave Thomas: Founder of Wendy's*, A&E cable television network, December 8, 1998.

2. Marilyn Achiron, "Dave Thomas: Putting His Money Where His Heart Is, the Man from Wendy's Crusades for Adoption," *People*, August 2, 1993, p. 86.

3. R. David Thomas, *Dave's Way: A New Approach to Old-Fashioned Success* (New York: G. P. Putnam's Sons, 1991), p. 29.

4. Ibid., p. 64.

5. Ibid., p. 94.

6. "Dave Thomas: Building a Better Burger," *Sales & Marketing Management*, May 1993, p. 52.

7. Linda Killian, "Hamburger Helper," *Forbes*, August 5, 1991, p. 107.

8. Achiron, p. 88.

9. Ibid.

10. Dave Thomas, *Well Done!* (Grand Rapids, Mich.: Zondervan Publishing House, 1994), p. 23.

Chapter 7. Wally Amos

1. Michael Ryan, "Why People Fail—and Why They Don't Have To," *Parade*, May 22, 1994, p. 4.

2. Wally Amos, *Man with No Name: Turn Lemons into Lemonade*, (Lower Lake, Calif.: Aslan Publishing, 1994), p. 20.

3. Timothy L. O'Brien, "A Cookie Maker's Aim Is to Be Famous Once Again," *Wall Street Journal*, August 16, 1994, p. B2.

4. Ron Harris, "For Famous Amos the Cookie Crumbles Just Right," *Ebony*, September 1979, pp. 54–56.

5. Mike Capuzzo, "When the Chips Are Down, Wally Amos, Father of the (Famous Amos) Cookie Never Gives Up," *Knight-Ridder/Tribune News Service*, August 3, 1994, p. 0803K3949.

6. Michael King, "To Sell or Not to Sell . . . Enterprising Business Owners Weigh the Question of Autonomy Versus Making the Big Deal," *Black Enterprise*, June 1987, p. 288.

7. Dana Canedy, "A Famous Cookie and a Face to Match: How Wally Amos Got His Hand and His Name Back in the Game," *The New York Times*, July 3, 1999, p. C14.

8. Ibid.

Chapter 8. Debbi Fields

1. Debbi Fields and Alan Furst, *One Smart Cookie* (New York: Simon & Schuster, 1987), p. 57.

2. Alan Furst, "The Golden Age of Goo: How Debbi and Randy Fields Unleashed a Cookie Monster," *Esquire*, December 1984, p. 326.

3. Fields and Furst, p. 50–52.

4. Regina Garson, "Cookie Dreams: And the Secret to Success," on the Internet at <http://minoritiesjobbank.com/women/womanpower/cookiedream199.html>.

5. "What She Forgot," *Nation's Business*, April 1986, p. 21.

6. Fields and Furst, pp. 85–86.

7. Alan Prendergast, "Learning to Let Go: Holding On Too Tight Almost Made the Cookie Crumble at Mrs. Fields," *Working Woman*, January 1992, p. 42.

8. Sandy Naiman, "Debbi Fields Is One Smart Cookie," *Toronto Sun*, January 18, 1999 <http://www.slam.ca/CNEWSLifeArchive/990118_cookie.html> (August 23, 2001).

9. "Mrs. Fields' History," on the Internet at <http://www.mrsfields.com/history> (August 23, 2001).

Chapter 9. Ben Cohen and Jerry Greenfield

1. Robert E. Sullivan, Jr., "Just Desserts: Can Ben and Jerry Make a Company as Good as Their Ice Cream," *Rolling Stone*, July 9–23, 1992, p. 75.

2. Kim Hubbard, "For New Age Ice-cream Moguls Ben and Jerry, Making 'Cherry Garcia' and 'Chunky Monkey' Is a Labor of Love," *People*, September 10, 1990, p. 74.

3. Fred "Chico" Lager, *Ben & Jerry's: The Inside Scoop* (New York: Crown Publishers, 1994), p. 1.

4. Claudia Dreifus, "Passing the Scoop: Ben & Jerry," *The New York Times Magazine*, December 18, 1994, p. 40.

5. Hubbard, pp. 73–74.

6. Calvin Trillin, "American Chronicles: Competitors," *The New Yorker*, July 8, 1985, p. 43.

7. Lager, p. 166.

Chapter 10. Paul Newman

1. John Skow, "Verdict on a Superstar," *Time*, December 6, 1982, p. 71.

2. Diane K. Shah, "Lucky Star," *Modern Maturity*, May-June 2000, p. 31.

3. Back copy from Newman's Own Ranch Dressing bottle.

4. Elena Oumano, *Paul Newman* (New York: St. Martin's Press, 1989), p. 252.

5. "Paul Newman's Dream-Come-True Camp," *Ladies' Home Journal*, July 1988, p. 34.

6. Janet Cawley, "Paul Newman: Still in the Fast Lane," *Biography Magazine*, April 2000, p. 50.

7. "Paul Newman's Dream-Come-True Camp," p. 161.

Further Reading

Aaseng, Nathan. *Better Mousetraps: Product Improvements That Led to Success.* Minneapolis: Lerner Publications Company, 1990.

Aaseng, Nathan. *Midstream Changes: People Who Started Over and Made It Work.* Minneapolis: Lerner Publications Company, 1990.

Bongartz, Roy. "The Chocolate Camelot." *American Heritage,* June 1973, pp. 4–10+.

Carson, Gerald. "Cornflake Crusade." *American Heritage,* June 1957, pp. 65–85.

Cawley, Janet. "Paul Newman: Still in the Fast Lane." *Biography Magazine,* April 2000, pp. 44–50.

Furlong, William Barry. "Ray Kroc: Burger Master." *The Saturday Evening Post,* March 1981, pp. 64+.

Graham, Judith, ed. "Amos, Wally." *Current Biography Yearbook 1995.* New York: The H. W. Wilson Company, 1995, pp. 16–20.

Graham, Judith, ed. "Cohen, Ben and Greenfield, Jerry." *Current Biography Yearbook 1994.* New York: The H.W. Wilson Company, 1994, pp. 120–124.

Graham, Judith, ed. "Thomas, R. David." *Current Biography Yearbook 1995.* New York: The H. W. Wilson Company, 1995, pp. 562–565.

Harris, Laurie Lanzen, ed. "Dave Thomas." *Biography Today, 1996 Cumulation.* Detroit: Omnigraphics, Inc., 1996, pp. 332–338.

Harris, Laurie Lanzen, ed. "Debbi Fields." *Biography Today, 1996 Cumulation.* Detroit: Omnigraphics, Inc., 1996, pp. 113–119.

Moritz, Charles, ed. "Kroc, Ray(mond) A." *Current Biography Yearbook 1973.* New York: The H. W. Wilson Company, 1973, pp. 230–232.

Moritz, Charles, ed. "Rudkin, Margaret." *Current Biography Yearbook 1959.* New York: The H. W. Wilson Company, 1959, pp. 402–403.

Moritz, Charles, ed. "Sanders, Harland." *Current Biography Yearbook 1973.* New York: The H. W. Wilson Company, 1973, pp. 374–376.

Skow, John. "Verdict on a Superstar." *Time,* December 6, 1982, pp. 68–77.

Internet Addresses

Milton S. Hershey
<http://www.hersheypa.com/history/milton_history.html>
<http://www.hersheytheatre.com/m1.html>

W. K. Kellogg
<http://www.wkkf.org/whoweare>

Margaret Rudkin
<http://www.cwhf.org/browse/rudkin.htm>

Ray Kroc
<http://www.mcdonalds.com/corporate/info/history/history
.html>

Colonel Harland Sanders
<http://www.kfc.com/about/story.htm>

Dave Thomas
<http://www.wendys.com>

Wally Amos
<http://www.northwood.edu/obl/1994/amos.html>

Debbi Fields
<http://www.mrsfields.com/history>

Ben Cohen and Jerry Greenfield
<http://www.benjerry.com>

Paul Newman
<http://www.newmansown.com>

Index